Luis Muñoz Marín

Community
BUILDERS

Luis Muñoz Marín

Community BUILDERS

Father of Modern Puerto Rico

by Linda
and Charles
George

Children's Press®
A Division of Grolier Publishing
New York   London   Hong Kong   Sydney
Danbury, Connecticut

Photo Credits

Photographs ©: AP/Wide World Photos: 12, 26, 29, 39, 42; Archive Photos: 9, 23; Corbis-Bettmann: 10, 16, 18, 22, 24, 27, 34, 38 (UPI), 43; Gamma-Liaison, Inc.: back cover, 33 (Larry Mayer), 6 (Jim Vecchione); Globe Photos: cover, 2; H. Armstrong Roberts, Inc.: 30, 36 (Alan Bolesta), 11 (W. Metzen); New England Stock Photo: 3, 35 (Bachmann); Robert Fried Photography: 41; Stock Boston: 44 (Joseph Nettis); Superstock, Inc.: 45; W. Lynn Seldon Jr.: 31

Reading Consultant
Linda Cornwell, Coordinator of School Quality and Professional Improvement
Indiana State Teachers Association

Visit Children's Press on the Internet at:
http://publishing.grolier.com

Library of Congress Cataloging-in-Publication Data

George, Linda.
    Luis Muñoz Marín : father of modern Puerto Rico / by Linda and
Charles George.
        p. cm. — (Community builders)
    Includes bibliographical references and index.
    Summary: A biography of a Puerto Rican leader who worked to improve
living conditions on his island, and served as governor from 1949–1965.
    ISBN: 0-516-21586-8 (lib. bdg.) 0-516-26513-X (pbk.)
    1. Muñoz Marín, Luis, 1898–1980—Juvenile literature. 2. Puerto Rico—
History—1952–   —Juvenile literature. 3. Governors—Puerto Rico—
Biography—Juvenile literature. [1. Muñoz Marín, Luis, 1898–1980. 2. Puerto
Ricans—Biography.] I. George, Charles, 1949–   . II. Title. III. Series.
F1976.M76G46   1999
972.9505'3'092—dc21
[B]   98-37338
                                                                      CIP
                                                                       AC

Contents

This tropical beach is located
on the Caribbean side of Puerto Rico.

Chapter ONE

Change Comes to Puerto Rico

What do you picture when someone mentions Puerto Rico? Do you imagine palm trees swaying in cool ocean breezes? Or high-rise resort hotels on sandy beaches? Do you picture an island in the Caribbean Sea, full of happy, suntanned tourists?

All of these pictures are correct. Yet, they do not reveal how Puerto Ricans struggled to make their island a better place to live.

7

Puerto Rico

Puerto Rico is a beautiful, fertile island. It lies about 1,000 miles (1,609 kilometers) southeast of Miami, Florida. Puerto Rico is located between the Atlantic Ocean and the Caribbean Sea. Its capital city is San Juan. Puerto Rico's area is 3,427 square miles (5,515 square kilometers). It is mountainous and enjoys a mild climate.

Puerto Rico☆

Thanks to the efforts of Luis Muñoz Marín, the first elected governor of Puerto Rico, the island is now more secure and prosperous than ever. He devoted most of his life to improving his homeland.

Luis Muñoz Marín did more than almost any other leader to improve Puerto Rico.

In the 1930s, most Puerto Ricans lived in poverty. Many were out of work. The only source of income came from growing sugarcane.

Most sugarcane plantations, or large farms, were owned by people who didn't live in Puerto Rico. The money these farms earned left the island. Puerto Ricans remained poor while people in other countries became rich from the sale of sugarcane.

Puerto Rico had few schools and almost no paved roads. There weren't many hospitals. At times, there wasn't enough food to eat or clean water to drink.

Slum areas like this one in San Juan were
a common sight during the 1930s, when most
Puerto Ricans were desperately poor.

Because of this, people didn't live very long.
The island was one of the poorest in that part
of the world.

Spain surrendered control of Puerto Rico to the
United States in 1898. Puerto Rican leaders argued
about whether their island should become a state
or an independent country. They spent so much
time debating the island's status, they neglected its
worst problems.

In 1938, Luis Muñoz Marín began to change everything. Luis thought Puerto Ricans should try to solve the problems of poverty, illness, and unemployment existing on the island. They could worry about the island's status later.

Luis formed a new political party. With the support of the poor and the working class, he was elected president of Puerto Rico's senate. He began a successful political career that led Puerto Rico into the modern world.

For a long time, Puerto Rico's sugarcane fields were one of the only sources of income on the island.

Luis Muñoz Marín's speeches were often broadcast
by island radio stations so his words could reach
as many Puerto Ricans as possible. Here his speech
is being broadcast from Caguas, Puerto Rico.

Political Parties and Politicians

Political parties are groups of people who share the same ideas about how best to operate the government of a city, state, or country. A politician is a person who wants to be elected to an office and work for the government.

During sixty years of public service, Luis transformed Puerto Rico. He led the island out of poverty with a program called "Operation Bootstrap." Working with the federal government in Washington, D.C., he improved Puerto Rico's official standing within the United States. While serving as Puerto Rico's first elected governor, he helped write its constitution.

Chapter TWO

Poet and Author

Luis Muñoz Marín was born on February 18, 1898, in the capital city of San Juan. His parents were Luis Muñoz Rivera and Amalia Marín de Muñoz.

Luis's father was already famous in Puerto Rico. He was a newspaper editor, poet, and statesman. He led a movement for independence from Spain. In 1897, Spain granted Puerto Rico the right to govern itself. Luis's father became head of the new government.

Spanish-American War

The United States went to war against Spain on April 25, 1898. Officially, the war was fought to help the people of the Caribbean, particularly in Cuba and Puerto Rico. After the three-month war, Cuba and Puerto Rico came under U.S. control.

In 1898, after the Spanish-American War, the island came under U.S. control. Luis's father left office, but continued to push for the independence of his homeland.

In this 1939 photograph, the American governor of Puerto Rico, Blanton Winship (standing on platform in dark jacket), addresses the Puerto Rican legislature.

In 1900, the United States government decided that Puerto Rico could have its own legislature, or lawmaking body. However, the governor of the island would be appointed by the president of the United States. Unfortunately, many of these governors could not even speak Spanish, the official language of Puerto Rico.

As a young child, Luis went to public and private schools in Puerto Rico. He loved to write poems and stories. When he was twelve years old, his family moved to New York City. His father was selected Resident Commissioner by the Puerto Rican legislature. The Resident Commissioner attended the U.S. House of Representatives, as a non-voting member, to speak for Puerto Rico.

Luis attended Georgetown Preparatory School and Georgetown University, near Washington, D.C. He studied English Literature and learned to speak French. During his studies, he also worked as secretary for his father. In 1915, Luis attended Georgetown Law School. He realized that law did not excite him as much as his writing.

Family Life

In 1919, while working as a writer in the United States, Luis married a poet from Mississippi named Muna Lee. They lived in New York City and in Puerto Rico. They had two children, Luis and Muñita.

After a divorce in 1946, Luis married Inés María Mendoza, in 1947. They had two daughters, Vivian and Victoria.

Luis Muñoz Marín, with (from left) his wife Inés and daughters Victoria and Vivian

When his father died in 1916, Luis returned to Puerto Rico. He soon went back to the United States, though, as secretary to the new Resident Commissioner.

Luis's interest in literature led him to write articles, poems, and stories for newspapers and magazines. In 1917, two of his books were published. They were *Borrones* (which means *Sketches*), and a work he helped write, *Madre Haraposa (Ragged Mother)*. He also became editor of a magazine about Latin American culture called, *La Revista de Indias (The Indies Journal)*.

In the 1920s, Luis joined the Socialist Party. He thought socialism could solve the problems of his native land. Ideally, under socialism, property is shared equally by every citizen. There are no rich or poor classes of people. It sounds good, but seldom works that way.

After a short time, he left this party. He joined the political party his father had formed, *Partido Liberal* (the Liberal Party). He also took over his father's newspaper in Puerto Rico, *La Democracia (Democracy)*.

Chapter THREE

"Bread, Land, and Liberty!"

Luis began his political career in 1928. At first, he was not too successful. He was sent to Washington, D.C., to get U.S. companies to open factories in Puerto Rico. Because of the Great Depression, however, companies didn't have money to invest in new factories. His mission failed, and for a while he remained in the United States.

In 1932, Luis returned home. He reentered politics and was elected to the Puerto Rican senate.

20

The Great Depression

The Great Depression was a period of financial hardship in the United States and around the world. In October 1929, many people lost their jobs and much of their money. Businesses did poorly, and thousands of banks closed.

During the Depression, Luis made many trips to the United States, seeking aid for his people. The Depression caused many hardships on the island. Friends he made in the U.S. Congress, though, sent millions of dollars to help Puerto Rico.

Customers line up outside a closed New York City bank
hoping it will reopen so they can get their money.
The Great Depression left many people with little
money to invest in places such as Puerto Rico.

Luis admired Franklin D. Roosevelt, who was then the thirty-second president of the United States. Luis supported Roosevelt's "New Deal." It was a plan to ease hardships caused by the Great Depression. The Liberal Party, however, didn't like Roosevelt or his plan, so Luis left the party in 1937.

Franklin D. Roosevelt served as U.S. president from 1933 to 1945.

Everyone thought that Luis's political career was over. But he knew what Puerto Rico need-ed. It needed a political party that really listened to the people and worked to solve the island's problems. He promised the liberals that within two years, he would win all of their supporters. And he did.

**Luis believed in talking to as many Puerto Ricans
as possible to hear their concerns and share
his plans for improving their lives.**

Most of the people of Puerto Rico were earning
very little money. Many earned less than $6 a month.
For years, political candidates had paid poor people
$2 each for their vote. That was a lot of money for
them. Most took the money and voted as they
were told.

Luis traveled all over the island in an old car. He drove through farm villages and city streets. He talked to farmworkers, fishermen, teachers, carpenters, mechanics, and others. He told them, "You can have justice, or you can have two dollars. But you can't have both."

Thousands listened to Luis. They liked what he said. He also found out what was really important to them. With their support, he founded a new political party in Puerto Rico. It was the *Partido Popular Democrático* (Popular Democratic Party, or PDP).

As its symbol, the PDP used the profile of a *jíbaro*, a landless farmworker, wearing his *pava*, a straw hat. The motto of the PDP was *"Pan, Tierra, y Libertad!"*, (or "Bread, Land, and Liberty!").

The 1940 elections surprised everyone. The PDP won most of the seats in the Puerto Rican legislature. Luis became president of the senate in February 1941. Luis worked with the appointed governor, Rexford Tugwell. Together, they improved Puerto Rico's economy.

They started a program to give land to poor farm-workers. They also improved the island's electrical system. Remote villages had electricity and running water for the first time.

Their economic plan came to be called *"Manos a la Obra,"* which means "Hands to the Work." An old American expression says, "Pull yourself up by your own bootstraps." This meant people should work hard to solve their own problems. So, in English, the program was called "Operation Bootstrap."

In 1947, the U.S. president was Harry S. Truman. He signed a bill, proposed by Luis, to allow Puerto Rico to elect its own governor for the first time

In this 1941 photograph, Luis Muñoz Marín (left) meets with Governor Rexford Tugwell to discuss ways to improve Puerto Rico's economy.

Luis Muñoz Marín took the oath of office to become
governor of Puerto Rico on January 2, 1949.
His wife (center) looks on.

in four hundred years. Luis was easily elected in
November 1948. He became the first elected
governor of the island. He was reelected three more
times. In all, he served fifteen years as Puerto
Rico's governor, from 1949 to 1964.

"Operation Bootstrap"

Important changes came to Puerto Rico because of Luis's years in public office. The most important change was "Operation Bootstrap." This economic program brought a lot of money to Puerto Rico. It raised the standard of living for workers. The island was transformed from "The Poorhouse of the Caribbean" to a showplace for other nations to imitate.

After World War II ended in 1945, United States businesses grew rapidly. By 1948, under Luis's leadership, expanding companies were persuaded to move to the island. Puerto Rico promised not to charge the companies any taxes for a few years

Puerto Ricans at work in a clothing factory, one of many industries that came to the island during the 1950s

if they would build their factories there. In addition, thousands of Puerto Ricans were willing and ready to work.

By mid-1957, more than five hundred new manufacturing plants had been built in Puerto Rico. They provided thirty-five thousand jobs and millions of dollars in income. There were chemical plants, oil refineries, electronics factories, meat-packing plants, and factories producing metals, plastics, and clothing. By 1986, more than 2,400 factories were operating in Puerto Rico, employing 200,000 workers.

Today, coffee beans continue to be grown on plantations in Puerto Rico. Coffee has become one of the island's major crops.

In addition to new industries, Luis's government started other programs to encourage Puerto Ricans to improve their lives. Farmers were taught to raise crops other than sugarcane, such as pineapples and coffee. Supermarkets, hospitals, and schools were built.

The number of doctors on the island doubled in only a few years. Before 1947, the average person lived only forty-eight years. Because of improvements in health care, diet, and education, Puerto Ricans now live to an average age of seventy-six.

Teacher training also increased. Before "Operation Bootstrap," only fifty-nine out of every one hundred citizens could read and write. Today, the number is eighty-nine out of one hundred.

Schoolchildren in Puerto Rico today receive a better education than their parents or grandparents received. This is a good sign that the island will continue to be prosperous.

Income rose dramatically. In 1940, the average worker earned only $200 per year. In 1977, earnings rose to $2,000. Today, the average Puerto Rican earns more than $8,000 per year. Puerto Rico ranks higher in average income than most other countries in Latin America.

Because of the natural beauty of Puerto Rico and the Caribbean Sea, tourism has become a major industry. Under "Operation Bootstrap," some of the most luxurious resort hotels in the world were built on the island. Harbors were improved. A major

Latin America

Latin America includes the countries in the Western Hemisphere that are south of the United States. People in most of these countries speak Spanish or Portuguese. A few speak French or English.

An aerial view of San Juan's resort hotels

international airport, located near the capital city of San Juan, was built. Today it is named Luis Muñoz Marín International Airport.

Another change Luis brought to Puerto Rico involved its type of government. In 1950, at the request of the Puerto Rican people, the U.S. Congress passed Public Law 600. This law gave Puerto Ricans the right to form their own govern-

Puerto Rico's constitutional convention met for five months before approving a final document on February 8, 1952. (Governor Muñoz Marín is sitting third from right in the front row.)

ment and to write a constitution—the first in the island's five-hundred-year history.

During the winter of 1951–52, delegates were elected for a constitutional convention. They were to decide what type of government would be best for the Puerto Rican people.

Luis and his fellow delegates valued democracy. With Luis as the main author, they wrote a constitution similar to the U.S. Constitution. In Puerto Rico, there are three separate branches of government. The bill of rights makes sure everyone is treated fairly, no matter what their race, religion, gender, or national origin might be.

Since 1948, the PDP had been in complete control of the legislature. They held almost every government office. Luis knew this was not good for the development of democracy. In the new constitution, he insisted a law be included to guarantee seats in the legislature to other smaller parties. Everyone was sure to have a voice in the government.

Some Puerto Ricans wanted U.S. statehood. Others wanted the island to become an independent nation. Governor Muñoz Marín knew that Puerto

The senate of the Commonwealth of Puerto Rico meets in this building, called the Capitol, in Old San Juan.

A Commonwealth

Like a state, a common-wealth has its own gover-nor, senate, and house of representatives. And, like an independent nation, a commonwealth has its own constitution, flag, and national anthem.

The flag of Puerto Rico

Rico was not ready for full statehood. But it wasn't strong enough for independence, either. He suggested a completely new kind of government— a commonwealth. As a commonwealth, Puerto Rico would remain part of the United States, but its relationship with the U.S. government would be unique. Puerto Rico would not be a territory, a colony, or a state. Its official name would be *Estado Libre Asociado de Puerto Rico* (Commonwealth of Puerto Rico).

Chapter FIVE

"Operation Serenity"

What sort of man was Luis Muñoz Marín? What qualities did he possess that made him a great leader for his people?

Between 1940 and 1964, the United States was led by five presidents. During all those years, Puerto Rico was led by Luis Muñoz Marín, first as senator, then as governor.

Luis had a knack for getting things done. He managed to unite people in Puerto Rico who didn't agree with each other. He could get them to work together toward a goal. To accomplish this for almost thirty years required special traits. He had a

37

Luis Muñoz Marín had a great talent for inspiring Puerto Ricans to improve their way of life.

lot of energy and intelligence. He had the ability to listen carefully to others' ideas.

Luis's education and study of other languages helped him get his ideas across clearly. He became famous for his ability to persuade people to join his causes.

Whether speaking to a crowd of factory owners or chatting to a farmworker over a cup of home-grown coffee, Luis was easy to like. His relaxed personality and the casual way he dressed made everyone feel comfortable around him.

38

Whether Luis was talking to farm-workers or politicians, his easygoing manner was always the same. Here he chats with U.S. Senator William Fulbright (right) in San Juan.

Awards

Over the years, Luis received many honors, including four honorary college degrees. He won the Freedom House Award in 1956, the Murray-Green Award in 1962, and the Cardazo Award in 1962. In 1963, he received the Presidential Medal of Freedom from U.S. President John F. Kennedy.

Idealists

Idealists are problem solvers who want things to be the best they can be.

Luis was an idealist. He wanted the best for Puerto Rico and its people. He worked hard and had the support of the island's citizens. The ability to listen carefully to the ideas of others made him quite popular with the people. He would take those ideas which he thought most useful and use them to reach his goals.

By the 1970s, Puerto Rico had been influenced by the culture of the United States for many years. A lot of young Puerto Ricans believed they were losing their cultural identity. Luis began to worry that the people of Puerto Rico were forgetting their Hispanic heritage. He wanted them to enjoy the benefits of U.S. citizenship, but also to keep their Puerto Rican customs.

For that reason, he started "Operation Serenity." This was a cultural program to educate the Puerto Rican people and enrich their lives. The program sponsored traveling libraries and cultural events, such as the Festival Casals classical music concerts. This annual event is named for another famous Puerto Rican, classical musician Pablo Casals.

Museums and art galleries were funded, including the Institute of Puerto Rican Culture. Scholarships encouraged the study of the arts. The program helped many young students make their dreams come true.

Performers at the 1998 Festival Casals in San Juan, Puerto Rico

In this May 2, 1980 photograph, mourners walk beside
Luis Muñoz Marín's casket as it is driven through San Juan
to the cathedral where his funeral will take place.

"Don Luis," as he was called in later years,
remained active long after he left public office. On
April 30, 1980, he died in a San Juan hospital. Puerto
Ricans, politicians, and other important people from
around the world mourned his death in a funeral
procession that lasted for twelve hours.

Today's Puerto Ricans have a bright future because of the efforts of past leaders such as Luis Muñoz Marín.

Luis's career had three main effects on Puerto Rico. His economic program brought the island out of poverty and into prosperity. He gave Puerto Ricans a sense of confidence and hope which they did not have before. Finally, Luis Muñoz Marín strengthened and gave new meaning to democracy for all the people of Puerto Rico.

In Your Community

Luis Muñoz Marín was a poet and a politician. He loved his native island, and devoted his life to improving it. He also encouraged the people of Puerto Rico to remember their Hispanic heritage. What can you do to learn about your cultural and ethnic heritage? Talk to

Timeline

1898 — Luis Muñoz Marín is born on February 18 in San Juan, Puerto Rico.

1905 — Luis begins school at the William Penn School in Puerto Rico.

1910 — Luis attends Georgetown Preparatory School.

1915 — Luis studies at Georgetown University.

1916 — Luis takes over *La Democracia*.

1917 — Luis publishes *Borrones* and *Madre Haraposa*.

1919 — Luis and Muna Lee are married on July 1.

1931 — Luis returns to Puerto Rico with his family.

1932 — Luis is elected to the Puerto Rican senate.

your parents about the ethnic origins of your family. Read about customs, celebrations, and other activities associated with your ethnic group. Visit a museum where ethnic art, sculpture, and history are on display. Write a poem about what you've learned. Be proud of who you are and where you came from!

Luis forms the *Partido Popular Democrático*.

1938

Luis is elected president of the Puerto Rican senate; Operation Bootstrap begins.

Luis marries Inés María Mendoza de Palacios.

1941

1947

Luis becomes first elected governor of Puerto Rico in more than four hundred years.

1948

Puerto Rico ratifies new constitution and becomes a commonwealth.

1951

1952–1960

Luis serves three more terms as governor of Puerto Rico.

Luis retires and returns to his seat in the Puerto Rican senate.

1964

Luis moves to Europe to write a book about his life.

1970

Luis Muñoz Marín dies in San Juan on April 30.

1980

To Find Out More

Here are some additional resources to help you learn more about Luis Muñoz Marín and Puerto Rico:

Books

Bernier-Grand, Carmen T. *Poet and Politician of Puerto Rico.* Orchard Books, 1995.

Chrisman, Abbott. *Luis Muñoz Marín.* Raintree Steck-Vaughn, 1993.

Fradin, Dennis Brindell. *Puerto Rico.* Children's Press, 1998.

Thompson, Kathleen. *Luis Muñoz Marín.* Raintree Steck-Vaughn, 1989.

Online Sites

The Latin American Network Information Center—Puerto Rico
http://lanic.utexas.edu/la/ca/other/pr/
This site is a reference source for links to many other sites about Puerto Rico's history, economy, environment, government, arts and culture, and news.

The Luis Muñoz Marín Foundation
http://www.flmm.com
You can read this site in English, Spanish, or French. Here you'll find photos of Luis Muñoz Marín, information about his life, and how Puerto Ricans today are carrying on his work to improve the island and its people's lives.

The Puerto Rican Hall of Fame
http://www.angelfire.com/biz/chago/puertorros.html
This site is a catalog of famous Puerto Ricans, from sports stars, to actors, to politicians. Includes photos, information, and links to other sites.

Welcome to Puerto Rico!
http://welcome.topuertorico.org
Visit Puerto Rico online. You'll find maps, scenic photos, and tours of cities. You can also read the Puerto Rican Constitution, sample the island's music, and hear its national anthem.

Index

About the Authors

Linda and Charles George are former teachers who have authored more than two dozen nonfiction books for children and young adults. For Children's Press, they have written for series including Community Builders, Cornerstones of Freedom, and America the Beautiful, Second Series.

Mr. and Mrs. George have been married since 1971, have two children, Christy and Alex, and live in central Texas near the small town of Rising Star. They enjoy traveling in their travel trailer to do research and gather ideas for new projects.